MW00966240

DAILY REFLECTIONS FOR LENT 2008
Walk With Jesus

ALFRED MCBRIDE, O.PRAEM.

ST. ANTHONY MESSENGER PRESS
Cincinnati, Ohio

RESCRIPT

In accord with the *Code of Canon Law,* I hereby grant my permission to publish *Daily Reflections for Lent 2008* by Alfred McBride, O.Praem.

Reverend Joseph R. Binzer
Vicar General
Archdiocese of Cincinnati
Cincinnati, Ohio
October 19, 2007

The permission to publish is a declaration that a book or pamphlet is considered to be free from doctrinal or moral error. It is not implied that those who have granted the permission to publish agree with the contents, opinions or statements expressed.

Cover and book design by Mark Sullivan
Cover image © John Foxx Images/Dynamic Graphics

ISBN 978-0-86716-861-7

Published by St. Anthony Messenger Press
28 W. Liberty St.
Cincinnati, OH 45202
www.AmericanCatholic.org

Printed on acid-free paper
Printed in the United States of America

INTRODUCTION

"Come, let us worship Christ the Lord, who for our sake endured temptation and suffering."

With these words the church invites us to begin our lenten journey that will unite us to the passion, death and resurrection of Christ by which we are saved from our sins and offered the gift of divine life.

Walking with us will be members of our parish who are preparing for baptism or for full communion with the Catholic church. We will pray for and with them. Their enthusiasm for Christ inspires us. Our perseverance in the faith encourages them.

The mystery of the cross infuses the forty days of Lent, just as the mystery of Easter penetrates the fifty days of resurrection joy.

The poor, the sick and the oppressed have found great comfort in the cross. The poor in spirit are attracted to the cross. The Man of Sorrows means a great deal to those dissolved in pain. The Crucified speaks to them when no one else seems to help.

The African-American slaves enshrined the passion of Christ in their spirituals. They knew Jesus could feel their pain in an inhuman world. When the soldiers put Jesus on the cross, they were there. "Were you there when they nailed him to a tree?" And Jesus was with them in their sorrows.

Jesus walks with us and helps us carry our crosses and make sense out of our pain. The secret is love. Reason has short wings. Love has an eagle's wingspan. The lenten liturgy is our angel showing us how to undergo a spiritual conversion through prayer, fasting and generosity to the poor. Lent does more than say, "Let us walk." It sounds like the more thrilling command, "Let us march!"

. . .

February 6
ASH WEDNESDAY
Joel 2:12–18; 2 Corinthians 5:20—6:2; Matthew 6:1–6, 16–18

Sincere Religion
Turn away from sin and be faithful to the gospel.

Ash Wednesday is a day of fasting. We are marked with ashes and accept the call to purification from sin and conversion to Christ. Our lenten program embraces fasting, prayer and generosity to those in need.

Jesus casts a searchlight not on the pious deed, but on the intention. If you want to be noticed, then don't do it. There is a confessor who often says, "For your penance do a kind act to someone without letting them know you did it."

Look for approval from God, not from the crowd. To seek public acclaim for our good deeds tempts us to pride. Piety's greatest pitfall is hypocrisy. The more you advertise your charity, the less love you really show.

Fast. Recall this adage attributed to William Penn, a seventeenth-century Quaker and American colonial settler, "Always rise from the table with an appetite and you'll never sit down without one." Fasting is good for the health of the body and the soul. Fasting clears the mind and cleanses the heart.

Pray. The greatest source of the Christian spirit is the Eucharist. Come to the Eucharist each day of Lent. Take in the

Bread of Life to quell temptation. Enrich your love life with the greatest love of all, the infinite love of Christ.

Help people in need. Millions of children are starving. Let us spend less money on food and drink for ourselves and give more to children in need. The breakdown of our excessive eating and drinking means a breakthrough for the hungry children of this world. Fast and you will get more out of life. And so will those in need.

Pray
Father, help us to hear your call to fast, pray and help others. Move us to spend time with Christ in the desert to meditate on the meaning of life and our final destiny. Show us how to get by with less, so that the needy of the world will have more. Amen.

Reflect
Be merciful to me O Lord, for I have sinned. How can I look at myself with utter honesty? When will I learn to say what I mean and mean what I say? How would God's mercy make a difference in my life?

. . .

February 7
THURSDAY AFTER ASH WEDNESDAY
Deuteronomy 30:15–20; Luke 9:22–25

The Cost of Discipleship
Francis Bernardone was born into a privileged life as the son of a prosperous cloth merchant. He fought in the wars between Assisi and Perugia. At age twenty-five he returned to Assisi, and during a visit to the ruins of the church of San Damiano

he heard the voice of Jesus from the cross, "Francis, rebuild my Church." He responded by following Christ's call to discipleship by denying self, taking the cross and following Jesus.

Deny the self. Francis' self-image had been formed around wealth and military adventure. He believed he should reform his life by denying his rich inheritance and commitment to war. His new self-image was focused on poverty and peace.

Take up the cross. Francis knew the easy life, wore fashionable clothes and was a minor celebrity in his hometown. He adopted a life of penance and detachment from the vanities of the culture. He became so identified with the cross that he received the gift of the five wounds of Christ, the stigmata.

Follow me. Francis imitated Christ so fervently that he has been honored as the man most like Christ in all of Christian history. His capacity for love and simplicity of life attracted all kinds of people to him. His celebration of poverty and mercy made him seem like a little bit of heaven on earth. His powerful witness renewed the Christian spirit in the Middle Ages and continues to inspire millions today.

Today's lenten liturgy summons us to discipleship every bit as much as Saint Francis of Assisi was. Let us pray to be disciples and let Jesus determine what kind of disciples he wants us to be. Let us let go of ourselves so that Jesus can live in us and that we can love others as Jesus did without reserve.

Pray

Jesus, open our ears to hear your three conditions of discipleship. Show us how to deny ourselves with joy and trust in you. Give us the graces to carry the cross. Light up the path on which we will follow you. Amen.

Reflect

Why is it necessary to lose aspects of self in order to be changed by Christ? How shall we let go of our fears of carrying the cross? When will the adventure of following Christ take hold of us?

. . .

February 8

FRIDAY AFTER ASH WEDNESDAY

Isaiah 58:1–9a; Matthew 9:14–15

Broad View of Fasting

Let the hands fast, remaining clean from stealing and greed. Let the legs fast, avoiding streets that lead to sinful sights. Let the ear fast, refusing to listen to evil talk against others and sly defamations. Let the mouth fast from disgraceful and abusive words. What gain is there when we avoid eating chicken, but chew up and consume our brothers and sisters?[1]

The above by Saint John Chrysostom is a broader view of fasting supported by our first reading from Isaiah.

Is not this not the fasting that I choose:
>to loose the bonds of injustice…
to let the oppressed go free…?
Is it not to share your bread with the hungry,
>and bring the homeless poor into your house…? (58:6–7)

The practice of fasting appears in other contexts and for different reasons, whether this relates to health or to social protest against evils in society.

Our health conscious culture favors fasting from foods that make us fat, increase our cholesterol or aggravate our nerves.

Millions of diet books instruct us how to lose weight and be healthier.

Mohandas Gandhi, a major political and spiritual figure of the twentieth century, used fasting as a nonviolent protest against mistreatment of his people in India. He would simply stop eating until the opposition gave in. Sips of water were allowed. Each day he grew weaker. The British government eventually gave in rather than make him a martyr.

While our official fast days are Ash Wednesday and Good Friday, there is nothing to stop us from voluntarily fasting at other times. Some parishes sponsor bread-and-soup dinners one evening a week in Lent. Additionally, we can undertake the more expansive practices of fasting suggested by Chrysostom.

Pray

Dear God, I see my sins before me. If you purify me in the sacrament of reconciliation, I shall be made clean. If you wash me, I shall be whiter than snow. Fill me again with the joy of your forgiving and helping presence. Teach me a state-of-the-heart morality, so that my heart will always be clean. May my various ways of fasting in Lent open my heart to receive your cleansing graces. Amen.

Reflect

"[A] broken and contrite heart, O God, you will not despise" (Psalm 51:17b). What is the difference between dieting and fasting? Why is the broader view of fasting as advocated by Isaiah and Chrysostom more useful? What is a good way to adopt fasting?

February 9
SATURDAY AFTER ASH WEDNESDAY
Isaiah 58:9b–14; Luke 5:27–32

Our Call to Be Holy

[A]ll Christians in any state or walk of life are called to the fullness of Christian life and to the perfection of love, and by this holiness a more human manner of life is fostered also in earthly society. In order to reach this perfection, the faithful should use the strength dealt out to them by Christ's gift.[2]

It's never too late to become a saint. Declaring, "Late have I loved you," Augustine did everything he could to avoid God's call to holiness. In describing his conversion, he pictured God as virtually yelling at him to wake up and come home.

You called and cried out loud and shattered my deafness. You were radiant and resplendent, you put flight to my blindness. You were fragrant, and I drew in my breath and now pant after you.... You touched me, and I am set on fire to attain the peace which is yours.[3]

Saints become holy. They don't start out that way. The same is true of us. In today's Gospel Jesus converts Matthew to be a disciple and to live a holy life. Matthew is a tax collector, a public sinner in the eyes of the Jews. Under the guidance of Jesus, Matthew will learn how to become a saint. Sanctification is a process that takes time and experience to transform us.

There is no holiness without love. Return again and again to Romans 5:5: "...God's love has been poured into our hearts through the Holy Spirit that has been given to us." Saints love God passionately and love people responsibly. The love that holy people use is a gift from the Holy Spirit. It is a spring that is never short of water.

Pray

Lord Jesus, you call us to be saints. "...[A]s he who called you is holy, be holy yourselves in all your conduct; for it is written, 'You shall be holy, for I am holy'" (1 Peter 1:15, quoting Leviticus 11:45). Conform us to your image so that we may do God's will in everything. Amen.

Reflect

How have you understood God's invitation to holiness? What are the consequences of walking the path of holiness? Why are many people like Augustine whose conversion came later in life?

. . .

February 10

FIRST SUNDAY OF LENT

Genesis 2:7–9; 3:1–7; Romans 5:12–19 or 5:12, 17–19;
Matthew 4:1–11

Facing Temptation

Mark Twain supposedly once said, "The only thing I have never been able to resist is temptation." People who buy the current myth that there is no sin like this laugh line. In laughing sin away, temptation, too, is just a joke.

Sin is no laughing matter. The cruelty that causes battered women, cheating spouses, traitorous friends or ruthless bosses produces no cheer in the human heart.

Who could gaze on the tortured Christ on the cross and then dismiss temptations and sin as grist for humor? On Good

Friday we betrayed, denied and killed our best friend. Some have revised the Golden Rule: "Do unto God what you have done to others."

Today's readings oppose the current political correctness. The first reading describes a temptation in the Garden of Affluence that leads to sin. The third reading pictures a desert of self-discipline that leads to grace.

The middle reading provides the meaning: Humanity's disobedience in the self-indulgent garden is reversed by Christ's obedience in the self-emptying desert.

Christ our God opens himself to the experience of temptation. His human mind and will are cleansed by the desert discipline. He feels the tug of the tempter and stands firm.

In each temptation he cites the power of God's Word. He is himself the Word made flesh. His victory is more than the result of human discipline. It is also a surge of divine power.

Today is a reminder of ourselves in conflict, drawn to sin as well as to God. Jesus permits himself to experience temptation. He shows us the two-pronged method for resisting the threat. The formula is as old as the Bible: a life of virtue and a relationship with Christ and his overflowing powers of grace.

Pray

Father of Light, penetrate the darkness of our minds that are unwilling to admit the reality of temptation and sin. Move us to accept the timeless truth about the destructiveness of sin. Help us face temptation as Christ did with discipline and reliance on divine power. Amen.

Reflect

What is the evidence in our society of the denial of sin and therefore of temptation? How would you develop the self-discipline to resist temptation? Why is grace also needed to fight temptation?

. . .

February 11

MONDAY OF THE FIRST WEEK OF LENT

Leviticus 19:1–2, 11–18; Matthew 25:31–46

Judgment Day

The altar wall of the Sistine Chapel contains the fresco of Michelangelo's Last Judgment. A cardinal objected to the nude figures and asked the pope to rebuke the artist. Michelangelo then painted the unclothed cardinal in hell. "Make him take me out," he fumed. "Ah, your eminence, I am only in charge of purgatory."

Every Sunday we dutifully recite this line from the Nicene Creed: "He will come again in glory to judge the living and the dead." Yet at some funerals these days the homilist assures the family and friends that the deceased is in heaven. The judgment of God is rarely mentioned.

Jesus is not shy about the reality of a final judgment. He tells us that we are accountable for our behavior on earth.

The criteria for entrance into heaven are outlined in the first reading in terms of fidelity to God's commandments. The guidelines in the Gospel emphasize that the way we treat people is actually also the way we relate to Christ.

God's laws are thus personalized. They are more than mere rules. They describe a relationship. To feed the hungry, clothe

the naked, visit the sick and the prisoners is to feed, clothe and care for Jesus himself.

The liturgy today calls us to examine our conscience. Am I more concerned about obeying and enforcing rules than caring for people? Yes, laws are important, for we do not want chaos in society or the church. But if we fail to see rules as ways of loving God and people, we miss the point. "[I]f I have all faith, so as to remove mountains, but do not have love, I am nothing" (1 Corinthians 13:2).

Pray

Hidden Christ, you visit me in a variety of persons. I admit I seldom think of seeing you in them. I tend to see you mainly in the sacraments and other holy realities. Yet you approach me every day for food, clothing, caring and a drink of water. Make me aware. Make me remember. Amen.

Reflect

Does Christ's judgment make me uneasy? Should it? If there were no divine judgment, how would that affect my behavior? How could I see Jesus in someone who troubles me?

. . .
February 12
TUESDAY OF THE FIRST WEEK OF LENT
Isaiah 55:10–11; Matthew 6:7–15

Praying Better

Escape your everyday business for a while. Hide for a moment from your restless thoughts. Break away from your cares and troubles. Be less concerned about your tasks. Make a little time for God and rest in him. Enter into your mind's inner chamber. Shut out everything but God. Speak to God with your whole heart. "Lord, I seek your face. I desire you," Saint Anselm says.

On the eve of his ordination, Fulton Sheen promised God that he would spend a holy hour every day of his priesthood. He kept his promise and wrote a chapter about it in his autobiography. He said, "This is the hour that makes my day."

What did he learn about the necessity for prayer? Neither theological knowledge nor social action is enough to keep us in love with Christ. Meeting Christ in prayer is needed.

Jesus prayed. Often he would go to a mountain or some secluded place and pray. His witness so impressed the apostles that they begged him, "Lord, teach us to pray like you do." His reply is found in today's Gospel reading.

He taught them the Our Father, the greatest of all prayers. It is God's Word coming into our hearts the way snow and rain water the earth giving seed to the sower and bread for the table. God's Word is always fertile and does not return to him empty.

Jesus wants to do for us what we cannot do for ourselves. He heals. He saves. He even dies for us when there is no other remedy. He shows us how to pray better.

The seven petitions of the Our Father lift our hearts to declare the holiness of God, a yearning for the kingdom and a surrender to his will. Christ moves us to ask for bread, forgiveness and victory over temptation and evil.

Pray

Come, Holy Spirit, and bring to us every word that comes from the mouth of God. Lead us into the solitude where we can have a relationship with Christ and pray the Our Father as he wishes. Amen.

Reflect

What helps you to believe in the necessity of prayer? What stories can you share about the power of prayer? How has prayer brought you closer to God?

. . .

February 13
WEDNESDAY OF THE FIRST WEEK OF LENT
Jonah 3:1–10; Luke 11:29–32

The Sign of Jonah

Scripture tells us that Jonah was a reluctant prophet. God had called him to preach repentance and conversion to the city of Nineveh. Jonah boarded a ship taking him in the opposite direction far from that city. God sent a storm that threatened the boat. The sailors woke their passenger to help save the ship.

When Jonah confessed his disobedience to God's plan, they threw him in the sea where he was swallowed by a great fish. Jonah remained in its belly for three days after which he was deposited on the beach near Nineveh.

Jesus cites the Jonah story today because it is a symbol of salvation. Jonah goes into the "death" of the sea, rests in the "tomb" of the fish and rises on the beach to bring salvation to a repentant city. What is imperfectly done in Jonah is perfectly accomplished by Christ.

Jonah is also an example of a man who first said no to God but eventually came around and did what he was asked. That is better than saying yes but instead just doing whatever one pleases.

Both attitudes linger in all of us. Sometimes we are reluctant but then give in. Other times we agree but then do what we want. Our maturing involves obedience to God's will in word and deed. Then the sign of Jonah becomes a reality in our lives.

Pray
Jesus, when you call me to do our Father's will, I need your help to connect my yes to my behavior. May I realize this is the way I live out your death and resurrection. Amen.

Reflect
What have been some "Jonah" moments in your life? Why is it so difficult to unite word and deed in one's behavior? Why is being a good example so essential to attracting others to our faith?

. . .

February 14
THURSDAY OF THE FIRST WEEK OF LENT
Esther C:12, 14–16, 23–25; Matthew 7:7–12

Ask! Seek! Knock!
Imagine Jesus crowned with thorns and carrying a lantern at nighttime. See him knocking at a closed door that is covered with weeds and old vines. There is no knob or place to insert a key. The door is locked. It can only be opened from the inside.

The artist William Holman Hunt painted just such a picture. He entitled it "The Light of the World." He took the idea from Revelation 3:20: "I am standing at the door, knocking; if you hear my voice and open the door, I will come in to you and eat with you, and you with me."

Our readings today are about prayers of asking, seeking and knocking. The inspiring prayer of Esther forms the backdrop.

"But save us by your hand, and help me, who am alone and have no helper but you, O Lord" (C:14).

But Hunt's painting reminds us the first movement of prayer comes from Christ. He enters our dark world with his lantern and looks at the door of our hearts—a door that has not been open for a long time. It is a humble pleading.

Christ wants a relationship with us. He wants to enter our home, sit down with us and have a friendly meal. He makes it easier for us to knock, seek and ask for what we need. Prayer starts with love. Prayer is linked to desire for God. The more passionate that desire, then greater is the power of our prayer.

> In my distress I called upon the LORD;
>   to my God I cried for help.
> From his temple he heard my voice,
>   and my cry to him reached his ears. (Psalm 18:7)

God knows our needs before we ask him. But he wants us to increase our desire for him through expressing our needs. The deeper our faith and desire, the greater is our capacity to receive the gifts God wants us to have.

Pray

> O LORD, God of my salvation,
>   when at night I cry out in your presence,
> let my prayer come before you;
>   incline your ear to my cry. (Psalm 88:1–2)

Reflect

What would help me to see prayer first of all as a response to Christ's reaching out to me? What experience of the power of prayer have you had? What is the value of asking for particular favors from God?

February 15

FRIDAY OF THE FIRST WEEK OF LENT

Ezekiel 18:21–28; Matthew 5:20–26

Forgive Until It Hurts

In the town of Nickel Mines, Pennsylvania, a man entered the small schoolhouse of the Amish community. He lined up ten little girls and shot them all. Five of them died immediately and then he killed himself. The grieving families came and picked up their children. They took them home, removed their bloody clothes, washed their bodies and laid them in clean pine coffins.

They set aside rooms with no pictures or furniture other than chairs where they could sit and pray and mourn. But just before this they went to the home of the man who did this. They told his wife that they forgave him. They asked her if they could hug her to console her. They buried their anger before they buried their children.

> So when you are offering your gift at the altar, if you remember that your brother or sister has something against you, leave your gift there before the altar and go; first be reconciled to your brother or sister, an then come and offer your gift. (Matthew 5:23–24)

The Amish families forgave until it hurt. They sought reconciliation even when they were the ones sinned against.

Ezekiel tells us today that God takes no pleasure in the death of the wicked. "Have I any pleasure in the death of the wicked says the Lord GOD, and not rather that they should turn from their ways and live?" (Ezekiel 18:23).

Lent is a season for mending fences. It is an environment of forgiveness. It is feeling the joy of God over the healing of old wounds. It is not the narrow and restrictive world of grudges about incidents eating away at souls who fail to bury their anger. Lent is a lot more like heaven where divine laughter rises when mortals reconcile.

We all have our regrets and hope that God is not staring grimly at our past. We wait for God's mercy more eagerly than a sleepless man looking for dawn. We do not wait in vain. God wants to forgive us.

Pray
Jesus, your first words from the cross were filled with forgiveness. You witnessed mercy in the midst of the injustice you experienced. Have mercy on us. Amen.

Reflect
What may be our failures to forgive? What stories of mercy have inspired you? Why so some people find it so hard to forgive?

. . .

February 16
SATURDAY OF THE FIRST WEEK OF LENT
Deuteronomy 26:16–19; Matthew 5:43–48

Love Whom? Your Enemies!
A January 1984 cover of *TIME* magazine featured a jail cell. Two men were shaking hands. One man was young, wearing a blue sweater, blue jeans and white running shoes. The other man, elderly, wore a white robe and skullcap.

Pope John Paul II came to forgive Mehmet Ali Ağca. The pope tenderly held the hand that held the gun that put a bullet in his stomach. For twenty-one minutes they met with subdued voices and occasional laughter.

After the meeting reporters asked the pope what he said. "That is a secret between us," replied John Paul. "But I told him I forgave him and assured him he has my complete trust." The pope also asked the Italian government for clemency.

"But I say to you, Love your enemies and pray for those who persecute you" (Matthew 5:44).

Once again the Word of God nibbles away at our resistance to forgive. We concede we should forgive our friends. But our enemies? That's going too far.

It is no wonder that the adjective that goes with revenge is "sweet." It simply feels too good. And if it feels good it can't be wrong, can it?

Christ would reply that, yes, it is wrong. Fix the picture in your mind of John Paul and his "enemy" sitting in a prison cell. That cover story appeared at Christmastime. Airport news stores lined their top shelves with the covers from end to end.

People try to argue for peace. And they should. But a picture showing an intimate act of mercy was obviously more persuasive. For a brief and shining moment, heaven's standards took a quiet bow before earth's querulous audiences.

Pray

Forgiving Lord, touch our stubborn minds and slothful hearts. Open them to your challenge to love our enemies. Make us realize that revenge is bitter and not sweet. It corrupts the giver and alienates the receiver. Move us to nobler acts that reveal the real truth about our humanity.

Reflect

In examining your conscience, who are the "enemies" you would never forgive? What is wrong with this statement, "Don't get mad; get even"? Why is devotion to divine mercy so fruitful?

. . .

February 17

THE SECOND SUNDAY OF LENT

Genesis 12:1–4a; 2 Timothy 1:8b–10; Matthew 17:1–9

A Life-Changing Event

On Mount Tabor in the Holy Land a church was built to honor Christ's Transfiguration. The architect commissioned experts in mosaics to do a representation of the Transfiguration scene.

The artists chose chips that would collect and reflect light. Hence when the morning sunshine streams through the clear windows of the dome and touches the mosaic, the garments of Jesus again seem to glow like snow and his face to shine as the sun. When the first streaks of dawn appear, the morning star arises in our hearts.

Intimacy between lover and beloved is a condition for change. In Scripture God humbles himself to lift up the hearts of his people.

Our first reading describes our God who steps down into the life of Abraham and rescues him from the dead end of having no children or a homeland. "I will make of you a great nation" (Genesis 12:2).

God walked cheerfully into the life of Abraham and Sarah and their extended family and bound them to himself in a covenant. God transformed them into the beginning of his chosen people.

Jesus fulfilled the promise to Abraham. In Jesus the Son of God became man and walked among us. On Mount Tabor Jesus revealed his inner glory to Peter, James and John.

His Transfiguration is a promise of our own life change begun in baptism and nourished by the Eucharist. The scene foretells his resurrection and ours.

God the Father tells us Jesus is his beloved Son and commands us, "Listen to him." Our process of transformation begins by listening to Christ. Yes, we should love, adore and stay close to Jesus. This will happen when we keep our ears open to what he says to us.

Pray

Transfigured Christ, we think of the face of Blessed Mother Teresa, the smile of Blessed John XXIII and the stirring voice of Pope John Paul II. They received the graces of your Transfiguration because they listened to, loved and adored you. Take us, Lord, and change us. Amen.

Reflect

What were three life-changing events in your experience? How would you allow God to change you to the person you were meant to be? What happens to an adult who ceases to grow and develop in faith?

February 18
MONDAY OF THE SECOND WEEK OF LENT
Daniel 9:4b–10; Luke 6:36–38

Forgiveness Is Not Rubbing It In...

…It's rubbing it out.

A little girl claimed she had a vision of Jesus. The bishop received a report about her case. He questioned her extensively, but could not shake her story. He sent her to a therapist who judged she was a normal girl with no psychological problems. The bishop chose a different strategy.

"The next time you see Jesus, ask him what I told him in confession." One month later she saw Jesus and posed the bishop's question. "What did Jesus say?" asked the bishop. "Jesus said, 'I forget,'" replied the little girl.

"Forgive, and you will be forgiven" (Luke 6:37b).

We seek forgiveness when we are aware of our sinfulness. The process of becoming a hardened sinner takes time. When that happens, we lapse into denial of our evil.

Our descent into sin occurs in five steps. The second sin is easier than the first. The more we sin the less we think it is wrong. In time we come to believe that sin is a virtue and virtue is a vice. Eventually we become hostile to virtuous people. Finally, we seek to destroy those who are good. That is why the infinitely good Jesus was crucified.

Our first reading is Daniel's prayer for forgiveness. To paraphrase: We are aware of the evil of our people. We have broken the covenant and the Ten Commandments. We have refused to listen to and obey the prophets. You, God, are a merciful and just judge while we are shamefaced for our infidelities. You are compassionate, yet we rebel. "We do not present our supplication before you on the ground of our righteousness, but on the ground of your great mercies. O Lord, hear; O Lord, forgive..." (Daniel 9:18b–19a).

Pray

Help us, O God of our salvation,
for the glory of your name;
deliver us, and forgive our sins,
for your name's sake. (Psalm 79:9)

Keep us from denying our sinfulness and give us the graces of repentance. Shower your divine mercy upon us. Amen.

Reflect

Why is it so hard for many people to acknowledge their sins? How do you benefit from the sacrament of reconciliation? Why is freedom from sin a cause for rejoicing?

. . .

February 19

TUESDAY OF THE SECOND WEEK OF LENT

Isaiah 1:10, 16–20; Matthew 23:1–12

Get Real

In Morris West's *Devil's Advocate*, Father Meredith is appointed to his last canonization case. Just before taking the job, he finds out he has terminal cancer. He asks the cardinal to excuse him because of illness. "Your real sickness is in your soul. You have never loved a woman, hated a man or pitied a child. You have not loved nor shown the need for love."[4]

Father Meredith acknowledged the truth of the cardinal's words. He accepted the case and allowed himself to be involved with the people he met. He brought hope to a bored, rich woman. He saved a boy from being exploited. He restored a priest's self-respect. Each of them gave him a feeling of being wanted and loved. He shed his role of being a religious functionary and attempted to be human and real.

Such is the message Jesus gives us and a number of the religious leaders of his day. They had made their faith a matter of externals. They wanted people to notice their works of piety: wearing large tassels, insisting on the best seats at banquets and requiring people to call them "Rabbi." They had become religious functionaries, empty shells. They did not love the poor, seek justice for the oppressed or inspire people with real humanity and sincere prayer.

The temptation to substitute external practices for genuine religion remains today, not just for priests and bishops but also for all the lay faithful. It's easier to obey rules than to build an interior relationship with God. It's simpler to be at Mass than to help build a civilization of love and morality. This is not an either-or, it is a both-and.

> What right have you to recite my statutes,
> or take my covenant on your lips?
> For you hate discipline,
> and you cast my words behind you. (Psalm 50:16–17)

Pray

Come, Holy Spirit, and give light to my soul. Show me how to be humble. Keep me from a merely externalized faith and move me to practice it in word and deed.

Reflect

As you examine your conscience, what is needed to be authentically a Christian? How have you seen this work in others? Why would this make you more truly fulfilled?

· · ·
February 20
WEDNESDAY OF THE SECOND WEEK OF LENT
Jeremiah 18:18–20; Matthew 20:17–28

Become a Servant Leader

Vanity of vanities and all is vanity.
The passion for power and money corrupts the seekers.

In the play, *A Man for all Seasons*, during the trial of Thomas More the turning point occurs when Richard Rich perjures himself to get More convicted. As Rich is about to leave the courtroom, More says he has a question for the witness.

"That's a chain of office you're wearing. The Red Dragon. What does it mean?" Chancellor Cromwell tells More that Rich has been appointed Attorney General for Wales. More looks into Rich's face with pain and amusement. "For Wales? Why Richard it profits nothing for man to give his soul to gain the whole world.... But for Wales?"[5]

Richard Rich sold his soul for power and money. In our Gospel we hear that James and John, encouraged by their mother, ask to be given powerful positions in Christ's kingdom. Jesus cuts them off from such corrupting ambition. "Are you able to drink the cup that I am about to drink?" (Matthew 20:22). Do they have the spiritual depth to endure rejection and martyrdom? Jesus tells them to forget worldly ambition.

That is a passion so powerful that no matter how high you reach, you are never satisfied.

Jesus reverses the current idea of authority as bossing others around. Leaders should serve their people, not push them around. "You know that the rulers of the Gentiles lord it over them, and their great ones are tyrants over them. It will not be so among you; but whoever wishes to be great among you must be your slave" (Matthew 20:25–26).

Jesus raised this issue again at the Last Supper. Instead of paying for a hired servant to wash their feet, Jesus did it himself. He instructed them to follow his example of humility and service.

Pray
Humble Lord, I think sometimes my ambition exceeds my talent. I enjoy giving people orders. I need the grace of being a servant leader. Grant me this, O Lord. Amen.

Reflect
How have I tried to achieve the ideal of service toward those for whom I am responsible? What often happens when I use force rather than persuasion?

. . .
February 21
THURSDAY OF THE SECOND WEEK OF LENT
Jeremiah 17:5–10; Luke 16:19–31

Develop a Social Conscience

[T]he story of America has been a story of long and difficult struggles to overcome the prejudices which excluded certain categories of people from a full share in the country's life: first, the struggle against religious intolerance, then the struggle against racial discrimination and in favor of civil rights for everyone. Sadly, today a new class of people is being excluded. When the unborn child—"the stranger in the womb"—is declared to be beyond the protection of society, a moral blight is brought upon society.[6]

Christ's parable of the Rich Man and Lazarus summons us to have a social conscience. Pope John Paul II often used the parable as an image of social injustice and challenged rich nations to help develop the poor ones.

The rich man in the parable wanted mercy after he died. But he showed no mercy while he was alive. He had no interest in the political and economic causes of hunger and homelessness. Worse yet, he did not even have the sensitivity to notice the homeless and hungry man at his doorstep.

Self-absorbed, he paid no attention to the needs of others. His belly was warm with food and his heart cheered with wine. He cared little about nourishing his conscience. He showed no mercy here so he could not receive any hereafter.

Though our culture is becoming more prosperous, there are still millions of children left behind, adults who are hopeless, the neglected elderly and disabled, people who seemingly have no social usefulness. Yet Christ is with each of them, asking us to help and love and have pity.

This scriptural teaching commands us to have solidarity with all people that respects their needs and supports the common good.

Pray

Lord of justice and mercy, help me to have a social conscience, to be willing and able to heal both the symptoms and causes of injustice. Encourage me to assist people's needs for food, clothing and shelter and a sustainable income that supports a family. Amen.

Reflect

What do you think it means to have a social conscience? What is your attitude toward the hungry and the poor? How do you treat people of a different race than you?

. . .

February 22

FRIDAY OF THE SECOND WEEK OF LENT

1 Peter 5:1–4; Matthew 16:13–19

The Rock and the Shepherd

Visitors to St. Peter's Basilica in Rome will see these words at the base of the dome, "You are Peter and upon this rock, I will build my church." Nearby they will see a dialogue also carved in stone. "Peter, do you love me?" "Yes, Lord; you know that I love you." Jesus said to him, "Feed my lambs" (see Matthew 16:18; John 21:15).

Jesus expected Peter to be a rock and a shepherd. As the rock, Peter provided stability, trust and continuity for the church. As the shepherd, he offered love, compassion and forgiveness to his people. He became a servant leader.

Jesus, the solid rock and good shepherd, supplied Peter with these gifts. The words of an old hymn would suit Peter well. "On Christ the solid rock I stand. All other ground is sinking sand."

Peter's pastoral wisdom is evident in his words to his fellow pastors. "Do not lord it over those in your charge, but be examples to the flock" (1 Peter 5:3). Good leaders serve their people. "For I have set you an example, that you also should do as I have done to you" (John 13:15).

These teachings apply also to all of God's people who are called to be servant leaders: parents, teachers and authorities of all kinds. Being rocks of stability, trust and hope, we generate confidence. Being shepherds of mercy and compassion, we beget a civilization of love.

Christ our rock and shepherd offers us these gifts through Word, sacrament and membership in his body, the church. Jesus desires that whatever is his may live and influence us. It is as though his breath is in our breath, his heart is in our heart.

Pray

Lord Jesus, we praise you for the ministry of Peter that abides today in the ministry of our Holy Father. We also ask for graces we need for our own calling to be rocks and shepherds for those in our care. Amen.

Reflect

"We do not live to ourselves, and we do not die to ourselves. If we live, we live to the Lord, and if we die, we die to the Lord; so then, whether we live or whether we die, we are the Lord's" (Romans 14:7–8). How have I been a source of confidence and hope for others? What do I need to be more compassionate? What challenges do I face when I try to be a servant leader?

. . .

February 23

SATURDAY OF THE SECOND WEEK OF LENT

Micah 7:14–15, 18–20; Luke 15:1–3, 11–32

When God Ran

"He ran to his son, embraced him and kissed him" (Luke 15:20b, NAB). This passage emphasizes the ecstasy of the father so overjoyed at the return of his prodigal son that he runs to greet him.

Rembrandt loved the parable so much that he painted the scene several times. His final masterpiece, *The Return of the Prodigal Son,* is one of the greatest treasures of the State Hermitage Museum in St. Petersburg, Russia. The huge painting occupies a space almost from floor to ceiling.

We see a bent old man and his kneeling repentant son. We feel the boundless love of the father and the regrets that it took so long for the two of them to reunite. The young man has squandered his money, his health and his self-respect. No matter, the inspiring message is that the father loves him and welcomes him home enthusiastically.

The son represents all of us in our sinfulness. The father symbolizes our merciful and loving God. The older son expresses the human unwillingness to forgive.

Usually the parable is named after the Prodigal Son. But it could just as well be called the Prodigal God who spends the wealth of his forgiveness more prodigiously than any sinner who exhausts his life and earnings.

Our religion is more than a balance between services offered and rewards obtained. The truth is more wondrous, for it is our encounter with divine forgiveness that invites our humble repentance.

Pray

Forgiving Father, you seek the lost son or daughter to enfold them in your love. Bring us home to your reconciling heart. Teach us how to offer that welcome to others. Amen.

Reflect

How strong is my faith in a forgiving God who makes possible my repentance? How do people overcome their unwillingness to forgive others? Who are good examples of people who have come home again to Christ?

. . .

February 24
THE THIRD SUNDAY OF LENT
Exodus 17:3–7; Romans 5:1–2, 5–8; John 4:5–42

Touch the Restless Heart

Bishop Fulton Sheen was not only a great preacher, but he was also effective in winning people for Christ and the church. One of his prospective converts was Clare Booth Luce, who was a success in the worlds of writing, theater and politics. She loved to argue and spar with Sheen, but he saw she had a greater need than scoring debate points.

During one of their sessions he asked her about the loss of her beloved daughter who had died. As she began to talk about it, she expressed her feelings and wept. Sheen then took her hand and led her into the chapel where they prayed in silence before the Blessed Sacrament. Her restless heart found a home. Soon thereafter she became a Catholic.

In a way that is how Jesus helped the Samaritan woman accept conversion. At first she was nervous, being alone at a well with a Jewish man she did not know. Jesus came across as a friendly stranger asking for a drink of water.

Seated by a well in a desert landscape where running water was as valuable as gold, Jesus said he could give her living water. More at ease she began to argue with him. Was he greater than Jacob who dug this well? Jesus maintained he offered water for a restless heart.

Then Jesus brought up her five broken marriages. She changed the subject and talked about the right place to worship. He said the day is coming when the Holy Spirit of truth will unite them.

She felt confident enough to say she sought the Savior. Jesus replied, "I am he." His divinity and hope suffused her soul. She left her bucket and went to her village to bring the good news.

This Gospel has a special appeal for those preparing for baptism or full communion with the church at the Easter Vigil. We all should undergo lifelong conversion.

Pray

Holy Spirit, we pray for all the graces and virtues the members of the RCIA program in our parish need for their journey. May all who feel the restlessness of their spirits find their rest in God. Amen.

Reflect

Why invite people to become Catholics? How effective is evangelization in your parish? What attracts people to your parish?

February 25
MONDAY OF THE THIRD WEEK OF LENT
2 Kings 5:1–15b; Luke 4:24–30

The First Rejection of Jesus

Prophets often meet resistance from their own people. When Jesus preached in his hometown synagogue, he met this typical opposition. The synagogue was a simple, unadorned meeting room for prayer and religious instruction.

The order of service included an opening prayer with sung psalms, a reading from the Bible, a sermon and a discussion. A religious administrator oversaw the ceremony. Jesus was the guest reader and preacher.

Jesus read from Isaiah 61 in which the prophet states that the Spirit of God anointed him to bring good news to the poor, the blind and the oppressed. Jesus read the text in Hebrew, then he reread it in Aramaic, which they understood. He looked at them deeply and said, "Today this scripture has been fulfilled in your hearing" (Luke 4:21). They were shocked at his identifying himself as the fulfillment of the prophecy. Yet they were also amazed at his eloquence.

Jesus reminded them that Israel had rejected the prophets. Israel had many widows, but Elijah only helped a widow in Sidon (Lebanon). God's people had many lepers, but Elisha only cleansed a Syrian. Jesus then said that even in his home area he will not be accepted, "[N]o prophet is accepted in the prophet's home town" (Luke 4:24).

His listeners then proved his point. They rose up in fury and tried to kill him by throwing him over a cliff. Jesus walked away unharmed.

Just as Christ was rejected, so will be the faithful members of the church. Our teachings on life issues, marriage and family as well as social concerns do not always get a friendly hearing in our culture. Sadly, even within the church this is sometimes true. In our lenten journey let us resolve to witness all the teachings of Christ and his church.

Pray

Holy Spirit of Courage, empower our wills to follow the full teachings of Jesus and our church. When we falter or fall, lift us up again. Let us take joy in following the difficult paths of our faith. Amen.

Reflect

Jesus did not fear to speak and witness the truth. What are some areas of my life where I fear to witness my moral beliefs for fear of rejection? Who are role models that would inspire me to live what I believe?

. . .

February 26

TUESDAY OF THE THIRD WEEK OF LENT

Daniel 3:25, 34–43; Matthew 18:21–35

Follow Christ With Your Whole Heart

We have …
     no holocaust, sacrifice, oblation, or incense,
     no place to offer first fruits, to find favor with you.
But with contrite heart and humble spirit,
     let us be received;
As though it were holocausts of rams and bullocks....
(Prayer of Azariah, Daniel 3:38–40a, NAB)

35

Francis Xavier Van Nguyen Thuan, bishop of Saigon when American troops left the city, was soon imprisoned by the communists. He was held for thirteen years, seven in solitary confinement. In the darkness of his cell he was not able to offer the sacrifice of the Mass, but he could offer the prayer of Azariah. He could surrender his heart and humble soul to God as his sacrifice.

He loved Jesus with his whole heart and wanted to love his jailers. He gradually showed concern for them, asking about their families, their anxieties and their deepest hopes. In time he won their confidence.

One day he asked a favor. "Could I have a bar of soap, a knife, a piece of wood and some wire?" Rebuked at first, he kept asking until finally they relented. He made a chain out of the wire. With the knife he made a little cross out of the wood. He sliced the soap in half and hid the cross and chain in the soap.

Several months later he begged for a little bread and wine, which in time he received. Then in the darkness he put a piece of bread and some drops of wine in his hand and offered Mass. He had no chalice, no vestments, no Mass books, just himself. However, the Trinity, Mary, the angels and saints and the church were there in the mystery of Communion.

Released from prison, he was made a cardinal and served in the office of Justice and Peace at the Vatican. His cell was his cathedral and his soul a living sacrifice.

Pray

Holy Lord, I may not always be able to get to daily Mass, but I can constantly make my life a sacrifice of praise for you.

Please make my heart and my body an altar of love for you and others. Amen.

Reflect
What paths can you take to make your life a sacrifice of praise for Christ? Why is the contemplative life of monks and nuns so valued?

. . .
February 27
WEDNESDAY OF THE THIRD WEEK OF LENT
Deuteronomy 4:1, 5–9; Matthew 5:17–19

Love the Ten Commandments

When the commission that composed the new *Catechism of the Catholic Church* completed certain sections, they sent drafts to all the world's bishops for consultation. When the draft on morality, entitled *Life in Christ*, was reviewed, prominence and priority was given to the Ten Commandments.

The world's bishops replied that the context should be Christ's two laws of love, the eight beatitudes and the vision of the Sermon on the Mount. The revelation brought by Christ is the better way of understanding the commandments.

Jesus said, "Do not think that I have come to abolish the law or the prophets; I have come not to abolish but to fulfill" (Matthew 5:17). Jesus taught both the spirit and the letter of the law and delivered fresh interpretations of the Ten Commandments. He personalized the meaning of the law and the prophets. Observing the commandments includes a covenant, a personal relationship with Father, Son and Spirit.

Some say that in our cultural context, laws and rules feel like curbs on our precious freedoms. But from Christ's perspective, his laws and rules are paths to freedom. We are free to do good. When we choose the good, we become freer. When we surrender to evil, we lose some of our freedom and even become slaves of sin.

Our reading from Deuteronomy today emphasizes the link between the commandments and the Lord God. They are the Word of God meant for the moral and spiritual development of his people. They benefit those who observe them. "You must observe them diligently, for this will show your wisdom and discernment to the peoples, who, when they hear all these statutes, will say, 'Surely this great nation is a wise and discerning people!'" (Deuteronomy 4:6).

Pray

Lord, Keep my steps steady according to your promise,
    and never let iniquity have dominion over me. (Psalm 119:133)
Amen.

Reflect

Why are the Ten Commandments valuable for our examination of conscience? What do you use to prepare for confession? Why are Christ's laws of love essential for keeping the commandments?

February 28
THURSDAY OF THE THIRD WEEK OF LENT
Jeremiah 7:23–28; Luke 11:14–23

Are You With Christ or Against Him?

...Make up your mind.

Thomas More's best friend was the Duke of Norfolk. One day they argued over whether or not to take the oath acknowledging King Henry VIII as head of the church instead of the pope. Norfolk was for it but More was against it.

Norfolk points out that the nobility of England were signing the oath. With some humor, More said that the nobility would have snored during the Sermon on the Mount. Norfolk pleaded, "Thomas, come with us, for fellowship."

Thomas replied, "When we stand before God, and you are sent to Paradise for doing according to your conscience, and I am damned for not doing according to mine, would you come with me—for fellowship? I will not take the oath."[7]

In every age of the church, Christians are faced with matters of conscience, with standing with Christ or against him. Lent is a time of discernment in which to examine our commitment to Christ and his teachings mediated by Scripture and the church.

More was beheaded for sticking with his principles and his devotion to Christ. John the Baptist stood firm behind God's law about marriage against a king who flouted it. The king ordered him to be beheaded and his head served on a silver platter to a young girl whose lustful dance seduced him.

Today faithful Christians in many parts of the world suffer for their commitment to Christ. Western culture mocks Christian beliefs and encodes laws that specifically oppose the laws of Christ. Europe formally has excluded any mention of the legacy of Christian culture in its constitution.

Choosing Christ is gradually going to be harder and the consequences more painful. This is the season of the Passion. Christ loved us to the end. Where do we stand?

Pray
Merciful Lord, I hear your call to return to you with greater fervor. Whatever sin I have, I know you will forgive me. Whatever troubles I bear, I believe you will console me. Thank you, Lord. Amen.

Reflect
What is separating you from the love of Christ? What can you do about it? When Jesus says, "Whoever is not with me is against me" (Luke 11:23), what do you think of his words?

. . .

February 29
FRIDAY OF THE THIRD WEEK OF LENT
Hosea 14:2–10; Mark 12:28–34

Hosea Celebrates God's Loving Fidelity
The book of Hosea builds its prophetic message on the loving fidelity of God for his people. Its first three chapters create an imaginary love story in which a faithful prophet marries an unfaithful wife.

They named their daughter "not pitied," referring to the fate of the unfaithful northern kingdom. They called their son "not my people," reinforcing the message that the northern kingdom is no longer God's people. Only Judah, the southern kingdom, remained faithful.

The prophet remains faithful to his wandering wife and leads her into the desert where she will be filled with the ideals that characterized God's people during their forty-year desert experience. "Therefore, I will now allure her, and bring her into the wilderness, and speak tenderly to her.... [S]he shall respond there as in the days of her youth" (Hosea 2:14–15b). In that desert retreat, she responds and returns to loving fidelity with her husband.

The story is an image of God's tumultuous relationship with his people. No matter how unfaithful they become, God pursues them like a fervent lover who wants a loving union again. The words of the popular hymn, "Come back to me with all your heart, don't let fear keep us apart," is based on the Hosea story.

There is a myth that the Old Testament presents a God of justice and the New Testament pictures a God of love. In fact, the two laws of love described by Jesus in today's Gospel come from the Old Testament. The command to love God is found in Deuteronomy 6:5, and the one to love each other is in Leviticus 19:18.

Fidelity is the test of love. Failures to be faithful undermine the relationship of lover and beloved. God's Word today pleads with us to be faithful and loving. We have a divine partner who never breaks his promises to us and always seeks to mend a broken relationship.

Pray

Faithful Lord, I need to hear your voice again reminding me that you want to feed me with the best of wheat in the Eucharist and honey from the rock of Scripture. Purify me and lead me home again to you. Amen.

Reflect

How do you feel when your beloved breaks promises? What do you do when you break your promises to God? Why is fidelity so important?

. . .
March 1
SATURDAY OF THE THIRD WEEK OF LENT
Hosea 6:1–6; Luke 18:9–14

Always Use Humble Love

At some thoughts a man stands perplexed above all at the sight of human sin, and he wonders whether to combat it by force or by humble love. Always decide: "I will combat it by humble love." If you resolve that once and for all, you can conquer the whole world. Loving humility is a terrible force: it is the strongest of all things, and there is nothing else like it.[8]

In his parable of the proud Pharisee and the humble tax collector, Jesus illustrates the best way to pray—with humble love. Humility alone is a difficult virtue to acquire. United with divine love, humility becomes a "terrible force" in the phrase from Fyodor Dostoevsky.

The humble publican beats his breast and uses humble love in his prayer to overcome his sins. Jesus tells us how pleased he is with this prayer.

The arrogant Pharisee puffs himself up with his imagined moral achievements. He thinks he is above ordinary humans who are greedy, dishonest, adulterous. Indeed, he is far superior to the hated tax collector hiding in the shadows of the temple. What's more, he is a top contributor to the temple treasury.

It does not occur to him that his gifts are from God and not just the result of his human efforts. He has a sense of entitlement. He is requiring God to hear his prayer based on his concept of himself as the only source of his good fortune. Jesus says simply that the self-promoter will get nothing and the self-effacing will be heard.

The words about humble love from the monk Alyosha in Dostoevsky's novel are a powerful application of Christ's formidable words today. Not only does humble prayer win forgiveness, it is a remarkable force in the struggle against sin worldwide.

Pray
Generous God, have mercy on me, a sinner. Purge my heart of any arrogance or self-destructive pride. Fill me with your incredible gift of humble love. Amen.

Reflect
How much insight do you have into yourself regarding the presence of humble love in your heart? Who are people who could inspire you toward this attitude? Why is humble love such a potent force?

. . .
March 2
THE FOURTH SUNDAY OF LENT
1 Samuel 16:1b, 6–7, 10–13a; Ephesians 5:8–14;
John 9:1–41 or 9:1, 6-9, 13–17, 34–38

A Journey Into Baptismal Light

The story of the healing of the man born blind was a favorite one at baptisms in the early church. Those Christians liked to call baptism the illumination or enlightenment. Catacomb art used it as a picture of baptism.

At the final exam for baptism the story was read. The candidates echoed the blind man's confession of faith, "Lord, I believe," and proceeded to recite the Creed.

His faith journey suited the process of coming to faith. The cured man displayed increasing insight. First he viewed Jesus as a man. Then he perceived him as a prophet. Finally he revered Jesus as the Son of Man, a title that in John's Gospel refers to Christ's heavenly origin.

This Gospel passage has the same dynamic value today for our candidates for baptism. God has enlightened their hearts and minds to come to the sacrament of salvation. The Holy Spirit has led them to the church and to the act of faith in the Creed. As they approach the font they are able to sing joyfully, "Jesus Christ is Lord!"

Cradle Catholics regain their appreciation for the baptismal journey by joining today's candidates in their spiritual enlightenment. The enthusiasm of converts reinvigorates the long-time members.

Young parents have another path to the same experience in the baptism of their babies. When the lighted candle is held near the child, the story of the cured blind man lives again. Not only is God's light in the baby, it is relit in the parents.

Our liturgy of baptism remains one of the best ways to appreciate this miracle of Jesus. Miracles in Matthew, Mark and Luke picture the joyful effect in the healed. Miracles in John also focus on the people's joyful experience of the healer. That is our gift today.

Pray

Jesus, Light of my life, stir up my heart to welcome your influence on my every thought, word and deed. Urge me to renew my baptismal promises. I will recall this each time I dip my hand in the holy water font and bless myself.

Reflect

What have been your experiences of baptism and the results for your life? What can you do to obtain greater light for your journey of faith?

. . .

March 3

MONDAY OF THE FOURTH WEEK OF LENT
Isaiah 65:17–21; John 4:43–54

Signs, Wonders and Faith

There is a difference between magic and a miracle. Magic is a trick, but a miracle is a mystery. Crowds seek out both kinds of events. There is a childlike pleasure in being surprised by a dove drawn from an apparently empty hat or someone mysteriously cured.

Jesus faced a similar psychology when he was asked by a royal official from Capernaum to come and heal his dying son. Instead of assuring the disconsolate man that his son would be cured, he commented on people's hunger for signs and wonders.

He wanted them to have faith rather than mere curiosity. The astonishment that miracles engendered too often satisfied people's enjoyment of the sensational and the startling. But it did not necessarily lead them to faith in him.

God had made a comparable point with Moses. "But I will harden Pharaoh's heart, and I will multiply my signs and wonders in the land of Egypt. When Pharaoh does not listen to you, I will lay my hand upon Egypt and bring my people the Israelites, company by company, out of the land of Egypt by great acts of judgment" (Exodus 7:3-4).

The nobleman was not interested in the misuse of miracles; he wanted a cure. He persisted in his prayer to Jesus, "Sir, come down before my little boy dies" (John 4:49). It would not be out of place to imagine Jesus pausing, letting silence precede his next words. Jesus was honoring the man's faith and wanted the listeners to note it.

Then Jesus assured him that his son would live. The man accepted Christ's words with faith and set out on his twenty-mile trip. Servants met him before he arrived home. They told him the joyful news of his son's healing at one in the afternoon the previous day—the exact moment Jesus told him his son would be cured.

"So he himself believed, along with his whole household" (John 4:53b). Sometimes faith precedes a miracle; other times the miracle evokes faith. In this case faith occurs on either side.

Pray

Lord Jesus, help me to have faith in you, not just for a miracle, but for having a deep and personal relationship with you. Show me your love and give me the love to respond to you. Amen.

Reflect

If you were asked to tell the story of your faith life, what would you say? What is your experience of the power of prayer? How is your personal relationship with Jesus growing?

. . .

March 4

TUESDAY OF THE FOURTH WEEK OF LENT

Ezekiel 47:1–9, 12; John 5:1–16

The House of Mercy Pool

We are all familiar with the pool at Lourdes where some people receive miraculous healing and most pilgrims receive a renewal of their faith.

Today's Gospel describes Jesus visiting a miracle shrine named Bethesda, which means *House of Mercy*. It was situated near the sheep gate through which flocks of sheep were led into Jerusalem.

The centerpiece of the shrine was a pool where miracles occasionally happened. Around the pool were five porches where the sick, blind and crippled waited for the waters to be stirred and a possible healing granted to the first one to get in.

Archaeologists have discovered the pool just as described by John. Stairways at the corners facilitated entry into the water that came from springs. Changes in water pressure may have caused the "bubbling effect" noted by the Gospel.

Jesus met a crippled man there who told him his sad story. He had been ill thirty-eight years, but never had help to get in the waters. Jesus asked him if he would like to be healed, and of course he said "yes." Jesus told him to get up and walk. He felt charged with astonishing new energy and arose and walked joyfully.

The religious leaders complained about Jesus "working" on the Sabbath. Jesus responded with a divine argument. "My Father is still working, and I also am working" (John 5:17). The miracle demonstrated his equality with God.

They saw his point about being equal to God and planned to persecute him for such blasphemy. He does what God does. To the ears of the religious leaders this is an act deserving of death. This would lead to the greatest of all his signs in John's Gospel: the Sign of the Cross.

Pray

Providential Father, help me to see your guiding hand in the ongoing work of creation. The heavens and the earth are the work of your hands. I praise you for your creation, and I adore you for the glory you manifest in it. Amen.

Reflect

As Jesus reveals himself through the miraculous signs in the Gospel, how does that help you get closer to him? God has made us stewards of creation. How do we fulfill this calling?

· · ·

March 5

WEDNESDAY OF THE FOURTH WEEK OF LENT

Isaiah 49:8–15; John 5:17–30

New Directions

God did not send the Son into the world to condemn it,
but so that the world might be saved through him.
(John 3:17)

Many years ago Katherine Anne Porter wrote a novel entitled *Ship of Fools*. The boat is a world in itself. The passengers come from all walks of life with their passions, tensions and struggles. There is the crew with their talents, training and responsibilities.

Suddenly someone arrives on board and says, "What you do is important. I have not come to change this or that. The problem is that your course is wrong. You are headed for destruction. I have come to steer you in the right direction. A great deal of your world, your life on this ship, is leading you away from God. I have come to swing this ship in God's direction. I can give you the strength to stay the course."[9]

Jesus is the rescue pilot that is putting us back on course as we sail on the ship of life. Faith means that we see Jesus as more than the greatest teacher of truth. He is truth itself. Our ship is headed for disaster unless we let him save it.

The wrong direction is our sinfulness. There is no way we can overcome our evil using our own resources. Sin is a condition from which we need to be saved. This is the truth of our situation. Jesus commands us to do more than consent with our intellect.

We must surrender our steering wheel—our will and our heart—that is taking us away from God and turn it over to Jesus, who is the real captain of our eternal destiny.

He has not come to condemn us from sailing away from God. He has come to save us because he loves us. He will never force us to surrender the steering wheel. Love does not compel. Love invites.

Pray
Jesus, Lord of History, we praise you for coming to us to take us where we will be truly happy, at peace and fulfilled. We cannot save ourselves. We praise you for our salvation. Amen.

Reflect
Why do people consistently think they can save themselves from sin and evil? Why doesn't Jesus just force us to be saved? How has Jesus saved us?

. . .
March 6
THURSDAY OF THE FOURTH WEEK OF LENT
Exodus 32:7–14; John 5:31–47

John Was a Shining Lamp
Most of John 5, which we are reading this week, summarizes Christ's dialogues with the religious leaders. Despite their murderous intentions toward him, he attempted to find ways to persuade them to be open to his teachings.

In our Gospel today Jesus looked for a way to get them to trust in him. He knew how much they had admired John the Baptist. Many of them had gone to the Baptist, confessed their sins and were washed in the Jordan waters.

They would have heard John's ringing endorsement of Christ and his mission. If the Baptist believed in him, why could they not do it as well?

Jesus also reminded them of his miracles, signs of glory. Through the miracles the Father had testified to his truth. Jesus gave them the evidence of the greatest prophet of the day and the greatest witness of all—God.

Yet these extraordinary witnesses did not persuade them. They knew the Bible, but they failed to see the living Word of God in front of them.

He saw how much they loved being praised by the people. Self-absorption caused their failure to believe. Glorifying the self is an attitude that kills faith. "How can you believe when you accept glory from one another and do not seek the glory that comes from the one who alone is God?" (John 5:44).

Jesus had tried to be gentle with them, but to no avail, so he switched to the role of fiery prophet. Strong language sometimes awakens the soul. "But I know that you do not have the love of God in you" (John 5:42). This terrifying accusation failed to wake them. They could not believe him.

Pray

Jesus, we believe in you. Help our unbelief. Give us the faith and love that assures a lifelong relationship with you that ends in being with you forever. Deliver us from every temptation to glorify ourselves with fateful consequences for our salvation. Amen.

Reflect

What do you consider to be the issues that weaken your faith in Christ? How could the religious leaders be so blind to the truth of Christ? What helps you stay strong in your faith in Christ?

. . .

March 7
FRIDAY OF THE FOURTH WEEK OF LENT
Wisdom 2:1a, 12–22; John 7:1–2, 10, 25–30

Kill Jesus?

Let us lie in wait for the righteous man,
because he is inconvenient to us and opposes our actions.
(Wisdom 2:12)

It's difficult for us to comprehend in our presumably enlightened culture that anyone would want to kill someone for religious reasons. Yet in the twentieth century, thousands were killed, tortured and imprisoned for remaining faithful to Christianity.

Speaking God's truth can arouse anger and opposition. Just before one of Pope John Paul II's visits to the United States, he was pictured sailing to America on troubled seas while some complaining Catholics shouted from the shores. But undaunted, the pope forthrightly held firm to Christ's teachings.

Jesus knew that even his apostles did not yet grasp his message. "For not even his brothers believed in him" (John 7:5). Jesus used plain and unsentimental language about the deadly effect of his preaching. He was confronting the power of evil in the world. They did not understand him because they had not yet faced such evil.

Our reading from Wisdom today remarkably describes the opposition Jesus was experiencing:

He became to us a reproof of our thoughts;
the very sight of him is a burden to us....
We are considered by him as something base…
and boasts that God is his father.
Let us condemn him to a shameful death.
(Wisdom 2:14–15a, 16a, d, 20a)

The whole passage from Wisdom is a prophetic picture of what actually happened in Christ's life and death. It is also a reminder to us that truthful witness to Jesus will require courage from us in certain circumstances.

As we move toward Passiontide, the last two weeks of Lent, we will meditate more frequently on the story of the passion and death of Christ.

Pray

Dear Jesus, you have taught me that not only do you have the truth, but that you are the living truth. Your life story tells me that commitment to truth is also dedication to you as my Savior who died for the truth that sets me free from sin. Fill me with your bravery so that I may have the privilege to walk in your footsteps. Amen.

Reflect

What kind of virtues will help you be faithful to Christ? How do you acquire the habits of the heart that tie truth and behavior together? When will you be ready to submit yourself to God's will?

March 8

SATURDAY OF THE FOURTH WEEK OF LENT
Jeremiah 11:18–20; John 7:40–53

Evil Plans

Today Jeremiah shares with us the news that his enemies are hatching plans to kill him. The Gospel echoes this theme by describing the frustrated plan of the religious leaders to arrest Jesus.

History is full of such stories. In medieval England, King Henry II was determined to eliminate his archbishop, Thomas Becket, because of Becket's defense of the rights of the church. In a secret planning session, Henry said to his barons, "Will no one rid me of this troublesome priest?" The barons obliged him by going to Canterbury Cathedral and murdering the archbishop in the middle of evening prayer. Becket was later canonized a martyr saint and Henry forced to repent.

There used to be a riveting radio serial that opened with the words, "Who knows what evil lurks in the hearts of men?" The question could just as well have been uttered in the pages of Scripture that reveal the true answer: God does. Jeremiah and Jesus confronted the evil that seized the hearts of those who opposed them. Jeremiah's sufferings witnessed the truth of his message. Christ's sufferings and death did more; they conquered evil and death itself.

Sin and evil have been driven underground in our culture. We hear of crimes and psychological disorders, but little of sin and guilt. Because of this the titanic struggle of Jesus against radical evil does not resonate as effectively as it should. Denial, however, does not eliminate the fact. Evil still captivates and corrupts human hearts.

This is a state from which we cannot extricate ourselves by any human effort. Only Christ's redemptive power can free us from sin and the attractiveness of evil. Faith leads us to be cleansed by Christ. The sacrament of reconciliation is Christ's healing gift to us. The Eucharist is the other side of the coin of salvation, namely, the incredible gift of divine life. Save us, Lord.

Pray
We adore you, O Christ, and we praise you, for by your cross and resurrection you have taken away our sins and given us the treasure of divine life. Amen.

Reflect
What do you need to do to depend humbly on the grace of God for salvation from sin and the gift of divine life? How do you benefit from the sacrament of reconciliation or confession?

. . .

March 9

THE FIFTH SUNDAY OF LENT
Ezekiel 37:12–14; Romans 8:8–11; John 11:1–45 or 11:3–7, 17, 20–27, 33b–45

A Sign of Our Resurrection
At every Catholic funeral the liturgy reminds us of three truths about the deceased. The beloved one's life is changed, not taken away. Our departed friend's soul is immortal. The body of the deceased will rise again. Scripture reveals to us that God has sown within us the seed of eternity.

In raising Lazarus from the dead, Jesus gives us a forecast of our lives after death. At the center of this wondrous narrative is the exchange between Jesus and Martha:

> Martha said to Jesus, "Lord, if you had been here, my brother would not have died...." Jesus said to her, "Your brother will rise again." Martha said to him, "I know he will rise again in the resurrection on the last day." Jesus said to her, "I am the resurrection and the life." (John 11:21, 23–25a)

The miracle is a sign of what Jesus will do for us in his saving power. By his death he will save us from sin. By his resurrection he will overcome death and give us eternal life.

We call the rising of Lazarus a resuscitation, a restoration of his earthly life. He died again at a future time. Resurrection of the body occurs at the end of our world as we know it. The church puts this story before us during Lent to strengthen our faith in Christ's resurrection as well as the promise of our own.

Modern technology cannot still the anxiety that death is the end of everything. Our faith responds with the conviction that death is a passage to another life—a life of joy with God.

God calls us to share in Christ's paschal mystery through a dying and rising with him. When Jesus saw the tomb of his friend, the Gospel says, "Jesus began to weep" (John 11:35). We, too, weep at the loss of loved ones, but this is a joyful sorrow tempered by hope in their salvation and resurrection.

Pray

Jesus, my resurrection and life, I thank you for the gift of resurrected life in the sacraments even before I die. Be my life. Be my love that conquers all. Amen.

Reflect

How do Christ's tears and trembling with deep emotion at the tomb of Lazarus affect you? Why is Christ's resurrection so essential?

. . .

March 10
MONDAY OF THE FIFTH WEEK OF LENT
Daniel 13:1–9; 15–17, 19–30, 33–62 or 13:41c–62;
John 8:1–11

Two Mistreated Women

Our liturgy today tells us of an innocent woman and a guilty woman exposed to death by hypocritical men. Chaste Susanna faced death because she would not yield to the lustful advances of so-called respectable men. The adulterous woman faced being stoned to death by men.

God inspired the prophet Daniel to save Susanna by exposing the lies of the unjust accusers. God's Son, Jesus saved the adulterous woman from the hypocrites who used her case to trap Jesus. If he disagreed with the stoning, he would be breaking the Law of Moses. If he consented to the execution, he would lose his reputation as a friend of sinners and a teacher of compassion.

Jesus used the strategy of silence to confound the accusers. He knelt on the ground and traced the dust with his finger. He initiated a reflective mood. Their angry breathing sounded awkward. His technique was like the sound of one hand clapping. He gave them no hand to clap against.

When the dust had settled, he said to those would-be murderers, "Let anyone among you who is without sin be the first to throw a stone at her" (John 8:7b). Jesus deftly moved attention from the woman to the men. One by one they dropped their stones and crept silently away. There remained a miserable woman and a merciful savior.

> Jesus straightened up and said to her, "Woman, where are they? Has no one condemned you?" She said, "No one, sir." And Jesus said, "Neither do I condemn you. Go your way, and from now on do not sin again." (John 8:10–11)

Jesus told her he knew she had sinned. With compassion, he gave her a second chance. He challenged her not to sin again. He made her feel that was possible. Jesus did not come to condemn but to forgive and help us repent.

Pray

Dear Jesus, we praise you for your wisdom in saving the sinful woman. We beg that same mercy for our sins. We accept your challenge to sin no more.

Reflect

How would you use the kind of silence Jesus employed in saving the sinful woman? How compassionate are you toward sinners? How does Christ's mercy convert us from sin?

March 11
TUESDAY OF THE FIFTH WEEK OF LENT
Numbers 21:4–9; John 8:21–30

Lifted Up to Cross and Glory

In modern times there has developed an optimistic view of the world. This positive attitude has grown despite Hiroshima, the Holocaust, the worst wars in history, widespread poverty, hunger and injustice.

Scripture also echoes this contradictory vision of the world. Jesus today says to those who oppose him, "[Y]ou are of this world, I am not of this world" (John 8:23c). In this version the world is not heaven. The world is transitory. Heaven is permanent.

But in other passages the world is the object of God's love. Genesis tells us how much love God exercised in creating the world and pronouncing it good. John writes that God loves this world so much that he sent his Son to save it.

At the same time there is the world that is penetrated with evil, with hostility to Christ. In this sense the world is the symbol of evil and all that stands against God. It is the arena of the battle between good and evil.

In the twentieth century the utopian governments—Nazis and Communists—preached an earthly paradise and outlawed Christ and the church. Their failed systems are their judgment.

The solution to the world as sinful is found in the passion and resurrection of Jesus. Recalling how the disease-ridden Israelites were healed by gazing on a bronze serpent raised on a pole, Jesus gives the real meaning of that mysterious image:

"When you have lifted up the Son of Man, then you will realize that I am he" (John 8:28). When Jesus is lifted up on the cross and from the tomb, then the world is regenerated.

Each of us is like the world in miniature in the sense that we are good but flawed, filled with potential but often prone to evil. When we have an honest view of ourselves and our worlds, we appreciate what Christ has done for us.

Pray
Hear my prayer, O LORD;
let my cry come to you....
The nations will fear the name of the LORD....
He will regard the prayer of the destitute.
(Psalm 102:1, 15a, 17a)

Reflect
What ways do you use the term *world?* When people use the name *world* as evil, what do they mean? Why does John say Jesus is lifted up?

. . .
March 12
WEDNESDAY OF THE FIFTH WEEK OF LENT
Daniel 3:14–20, 91–92, 95; John 8:31–42

Be Not Afraid
We normally think the opposite of love is hate, and in one sense it is. But psychologically speaking, fear is the opposite of love. Throughout all of Lent Jesus is showing us his love in a variety of ways. Do we still resist Christ's love? Fear drives out love.

Accepting redeeming love requires responsible living and that causes us to pause and be afraid. The life of faith is filled with challenges that frighten us. We need to keep repeating what Jesus and Pope John Paul the Beloved said to us: "Be not afraid."

Every time heaven touches earth, angels ease us with words that banish fear. Fear is the stumbling block of love. Imagine the fear of the three young friends. The king condemns them to walk into a wall of fire if they insist on being faithful to God.

In ancient times, a trial by fire was sometimes used to test the integrity of people. Some were forced to walk on burning coals. Others were compelled to lift a heavy stone out of boiling water. The three young men proved their love for God by walking into a wall of fire.

They had fear. But their love was greater. They sang the praises of God in that fearful inferno. The guard told the king, "I see four men, unfettered and unhurt walking in the fire, and the fourth looks like a son of God" (Daniel 3:92, NAB). When we walk in faith and love, Jesus throws away our fear and walks with us. Love will cast out your fear.

Pray
Lord Jesus, flood my soul with the love that casts out fear. Help me to realize that even if I do not see what's ahead I will be safe with you because you lead me. Amen.

Reflect
In matters of faith, what do you fear? In issues of love what makes you afraid? If your fear is gone how did that happen?

. . .

March 13

THURSDAY OF THE FIFTH WEEK OF LENT

Genesis 17:3–9; John 8:51–59

Before Abraham, I Am

Russian icons bring Scripture scenes to life in a spiritual and inviting manner. One of them, titled "The Hospitality of Abraham," pictures Abraham and Sarah in the background holding platters of food. In the foreground are three visitors from heaven. One of the greatest icons, painted by Andre Rublev in 1411, it is also known as "The Old Testament Trinity." Abraham's three guests sit around a stone table that looks like an altar. On the table is a gold chalice filled with red wine and bread. The Eastern churches prepare the Eucharist this way and people receive Christ's body and blood from a spoon.

Rublev did not specify the identity of the persons in order to emphasize the unity in the Trinity. However, the Father and the Son and the Spirit are there. In today's Gospel Jesus speaks warmly and with familiarity about his knowledge of his Father.

He refers to the hospitality of Abraham. "Abraham rejoiced that he would see my day; he saw it and was glad" (John 8:56). His listeners complained that this was impossible, for Jesus was not yet fifty! Recalling fondly his dinner at the home of Abraham, Jesus said, "[B]efore Abraham was, I am" (John 8:58). At this confession of his divinity, Jesus departed the temple grounds just as his enemies picked up stones to kill him.

Jesus repeatedly made it clear that the test of faith was seen in the way people received him. Jesus is central to the world's history and the life of every man and woman. People keep finding new ways to eliminate Jesus from his key role as Savior.

They have used murder, ridicule and cynical indifference, but Jesus cannot be ignored. He is always the Tremendous Lover who reaches out to every human heart. Our response is simple though hard for many to make. A yes to Christ opens us to salvation.

Pray
Divine Lord and Savior, we believe in you, but help our unbelief. So many distractions pull us away from the best of all relationships, a loving friendship with you. Grant us a heart that welcomes you at every minute. Amen.

Reflect
What helps you keep your faith in the divinity of Christ? What keeps you in touch with Jesus our Savior? How are you sharing your faith with others?

. . .

March 14
FRIDAY OF THE FIFTH WEEK OF LENT
Jeremiah 20:10–13; John 10:31–42

Adult Faith
There are three major stages in faith development: the child, the teen and the adult. The child with simplicity and wonder accepts the mystery of God with joy and even playfulness. The teen rightly questions how the mystery of God fits with all the world's problems and challenges. The challenge for the teen is to grow up.

The adult finally settles on and is comfortable with God as a mystery. Adoration, love and prayer serve the adult's relationship with God. Questions remain as to how other matters relate to the mystery, but the mystery itself is sacrosanct.

Jeremiah comes to us today surrounded by terrors on every side. Political and religious leaders form a coalition of the hostile against him. Even his friends watch for ways to trip him up. The mature faith of Jeremiah withstands such tempests. "But the LORD is with me like a dread warrior" (Jeremiah 20:11). The prophet has analyzed his anxieties and the threats of others, and in his distress he called upon the Lord who listened to his voice. His cry reached the ears of God who gave him the safety he desired.

Jesus, too, is surrounded by threats of death, misunderstanding and accusations of blasphemy. But Christ is rooted in the mystery of God and is indeed the very mystery of God. "[T]he Father is in me and I am in the Father" (John 10:38). There is no disconnect between his words and deeds. He challenges his adversaries to believe his deeds and words.

Today everyone believes they have a right to talk about religion as though they were religious. They go on talk shows and pontificate about the most sacred topics. They do not seem to notice how careless they are. God is not a mystery to them, not a sublime source of beauty and truth. They tamper when they should be reverent. Adult faith is our reply. We raise our voices in prayer and trust that God, from his holy temple, will hear us.

Pray

Heavenly Father, in the midst of life's troubles, we cry out to you. When the waves of destruction surge about us, we praise you for your salvation. Amen.

Reflect

How adult is your faith? How mature is your relationship with God? How do we keep on growing in faith?

. . .

March 15

SATURDAY OF THE FIFTH WEEK OF LENT

2 Samuel 7:4–5a, 12–14a, 16; Romans 4:13, 16–18, 22;
Matthew 1:16, 18–21, 24 or Luke 2:41–51a

Joseph's Dream

Twentieth-century Swiss psychiatrist Carl Jung considered dreams to be a rich source of interpreting the lives of his clients. In many parts of Scripture God uses dreams to help his followers understand his plans. To solve Joseph's dilemma caused by Mary's unexpected pregnancy an angel appeared to him in a dream. The heavenly counselor reassured Joseph that Mary's pregnancy was the result of the work of the Holy Spirit.

Jewish marriage customs attached a greater importance to the engagement ceremony than does our modern society. In effect the engagement was like the beginning of the marital commitment, though sexual privileges were deferred until after the marriage ceremony.

Joseph was upset, but he was a righteous man who did not want to publicly shame Mary. He planned to end their relationship quietly. As an observer of the law, he felt bound to terminate the engagement, but as a sensitive and compassionate man he sought a private settlement.

After hearing the message of the angel that the child was conceived by the Spirit and would be born of a virginal Mary, Joseph's heart was opened to God's plan. When Joseph awoke, he did what the angel commanded and took Mary as his wife into his home.

Joseph continued to be a pure, gentle, prudent husband and a stepfather of Jesus. He modeled faith and obedience for Jesus, brought him to synagogue and temple and taught him carpentry. A surprising dream had come true in his life in which he would live with the Mother of God and God's own Son.

Pray
Loving Father, I praise you for the sensitivity and faith Joseph showed to Blessed Mary. I pray for an understanding and forgiving nature whenever I face someone with whom I do not get along. Dear Father, help me when I have difficulty believing in you. Amen.

Reflect
Who are some inspiring couples you know who have overcome difficulties in their marriages? When you think of someone who is a good father to his children, what qualities come to your mind? How can Saint Joseph be of help to you?

. . .

March 16
PALM SUNDAY OF THE LORD'S PASSION
Matthew 21:1–11; Isaiah 50:4–7; Philippians 2:6–11;
Matthew 26:14—27:66 or 27:11–54

Behold the Wondrous Cross
In the year 1224 Saint Francis of Assisi went to Mount LaVerna to fast and pray for forty days in preparation for the feast of the Exaltation of the Holy Cross. He asked Brother Leo to choose

Scripture texts for his meditation. Leo selected passages from the Passion narratives. In a dream during his retreat, Francis heard an angel play a violin as it is heard before God. Its one note was so beautiful that Francis felt he was already in heaven.

At midnight on the eve of the feast, Francis prayed for two favors: "I want to feel the pain of Christ in his passion. I ask for the love that moved Jesus to die for our salvation." A vision of fire came from heaven. In its midst was the crucified Christ. The image touched Francis and imprinted Christ's five wounds on him. In his heart he felt pure, divine love.

As we begin Holy Week, Saint Francis reminds us to do more than look at the cross. We see the external cause of pain. We need to look for the interior love that accepted the pain and gave it meaning. We must welcome the cross Jesus offers us and the love that gives it meaning.

Christ's cross stands between the Hosannas of Palm Sunday and Alleluias of Easter and in front of the curses of the mob on Good Friday. The contradictions and paradoxes are all part of the picture. They will be part of our life story too. Jesus has been there.

In the new Los Angeles cathedral the crucifix behind the altar is a great attraction for Hispanic worshipers. So many of whom have kissed Christ's feet after Mass that the surface is wearing away. It is a tribute to Christ's greatest act of love.

Pray

Crucified Lord, when I survey your wondrous cross, all that I have gained materially in life is nothing in comparison to your sacrificial love. Lead me to respond with all my heart. Amen.

Reflect

How do you keep loving God and other people even when it seems too difficult? Who are some people you know who carry their crosses with prayer and dignity? What does Palm Sunday say to you?

. . .

March 17
MONDAY OF HOLY WEEK
Isaiah 42:1–7; John 12:1–11

The Friends of Jesus

On the Monday before he died, Jesus went to a dinner party in Bethany at the home of Martha, Mary and Lazarus. Martha cooked a festive meal. Family and friends celebrated the resurrection of Lazarus. Jesus sat next to the man risen from the dead.

In the midst of that joyful occasion, Mary knelt before Jesus, took a jar of expensive perfume and exuberantly poured all of its contents on Jesus' feet. Mary illustrated the generosity of love. The lover gives everything to the beloved. The price may be big or small. If the price is small, but it is all one has, then it is total giving.

Judas complained that Mary wasted what would have been a worker's wages for a year. Better to have given the money to the poor. Judas was a thief who stole money from the apostles' purse. The cheerful group at Bethany was not greedy. They needed no reminder to help the poor and saw no contradiction between Mary's extravagant gift and their moral obligations to the needy. Jesus rebuked Judas. "Leave her alone" (John 12:7). Mysteriously he added that Mary had anointed him for his burial. That evening was a time for loving him before he died.

We should always love and help the poor. But we should also love and serve those who are near and dear to us while we have the time. Too many regret at gravesides how much they should have done for the departed one when alive.

Jesus returned a spirit of joy to that pleasant gathering, though his words about his burial left a sense of unease. As we gaze on that scene, we look more deeply at a man returned from the dead and Christ who would be in a grave in less than six days. His beloved Martha and Mary stand like angels at his side. They were his friends when he needed them most.

Pray
Jesus, friend of Martha, Mary and Lazarus, we ask of you the gift of friendship. Speak to us your words at the Last Supper, "I have called you friends" (John 15:15). Bring us closer to you each day. Amen.

Reflect
What experiences have deepened your friendship with Christ? Why is a relationship with Jesus essential for you?

. . .
March 18
TUESDAY OF HOLY WEEK
Isaiah 49:1–6; John 13:21–33, 36–38

One of You Will Betray Me
One of the historic meanings of the Passover meal was that it was meant to be a friendship meal. Through its celebration the diners would receive the gift of reconciliation with each other

from God. When Da Vinci painted the Last Supper, he concentrated on the reaction of the apostles to Christ's words that one of them would betray him.

Da Vinci captured the shock of the apostles at hearing one of them was a traitor when it was assumed they were all friends. Commentaries on the painting dwell on the various ways the men reacted. The practical-minded Peter gestured to John to ask Jesus who it was.

Jesus had no intention of revealing or exposing Judas to the sudden anger of the apostolic band. He did not want the meal to become a brawl. The beloved disciple is told who it is but that was for his ears alone. John saw in Christ's dipping some bread into the dish and handing it to Judas a gesture of friendship. At that moment Satan entered into Judas. Jesus told him, "Do quickly what you are going to do" (John 13:27). None at table understood what this meant. The scene concludes with the symbolic words, "And it was night" (John 13:30).

The act of Judas was so awful, coming as it did at the first Eucharist, that it has never been forgotten by the church. In Eucharistic Prayer III it is remembered, "On the night he was betrayed…" Those jarring words still unsettle worshipers.

The most beautiful of all the sacraments retains a painful memory, not just as a tribute to the facts of the matter, but as a caution to all who come to the Holy Table. Faithful believers need to recall their forgiveness and maintain vigilance.

Pray

O Lord, be merciful to me, a sinner. Put a guard over my mouth that no sinful words emerge, and over my deeds that sins do not mar them. Purify me, as I am not worthy to receive you. Amen.

Reflect

In what sense might you think you have "betrayed" Jesus? Why must we come to the table of the Lord with a clean heart? Why should we preserve our friendship with God and each other?

· · ·

March 19

WEDNESDAY OF HOLY WEEK

Isaiah 50:4–9a; Matthew 26:14–25

Darkness Descends

> Now when I was alone, and had no one in whose company I could find relaxation, I was unable to pray or read.… I was like this for four or five hours, and neither in Heaven nor on earth was there any comfort for me.… O my Lord, how true a friend Thou art, and how powerful! For Thou canst do all Thou wilt and never dost Thou cease to will if we love Thee.[10]

Teresa of Avila experienced darkness in her journey to God. She understood that it was part of her spiritual maturing and purification. That doesn't make it any easier to bear. But she always found confidence to go on by returning again and again to her true friend, Jesus, who wants to be with her in such times of trouble.

Our liturgy dwells again on the betrayal of Christ by Judas. Darkness descends on Jesus. He knows what will happen. He does not run away from the cross. The words of Isaiah apply perfectly to what is about to happen to Christ. "I gave my back to those who struck me, / and my cheeks to those who pulled out the beard; / I did not hide my face from insult and spitting" (Isaiah 50:6).

Jesus takes on our human nature so he can experience the effects of the sinfulness it brings: loneliness, betrayal, injustice, abandonment by friends, physical and psychological pain. At the same time, by his divinity he brings to us redemption from sin and its effects. He is more intimate with us than we are with ourselves. Teresa is right. In the midst of our sea of troubles we should hasten to be with Jesus.

The liturgy brings us to the table of the Last Supper on Tuesday, Wednesday and Thursday of Holy Week. Two of those days we bear with him the sorrow of betrayal. On Holy Thursday we celebrate the glory of his institution of the Holy Eucharist, the Sacrament of Love, which is the door to sanctification.

Pray
We adore you, O Christ, and we praise you, for in the Eucharist you have given us the fruits of your cross and resurrection.

Reflect
How can you praise Christ for his redemptive gifts? In what ways do you open your heart to Christ your friend?

. . .
March 20
HOLY THURSDAY
Chrism Mass: Isaiah 61:1–3a, 6a, 8b–9,
Revelation 1:5–8, Luke 4:16–21
Evening Mass of the Lord's Supper: Exodus 12:1–8, 11–14;
1 Corinthians 11:23–26; John 13:1–15

The Sacrament of Love

Eat this sacred food
so that your bond of unity with Christ may never be broken.
Drink this sacred blood, the price he paid for you,
so that you may never lose heart because of your sinfulness.[11]

It is impossible in human words to express adequately the joy that comes from celebrating this Sacrament of Love. Pope Benedict XVI used this phrase as the title of his apostolic exhortation on the Eucharist. Our Holy Thursday liturgy places Christ's words of institution of the Eucharist between the memory of the first Passover meal and the touching scene of Christ washing the feet of his apostles.

At the Last Supper Jesus transformed the ancient Passover into the new Passover of the Eucharist that makes present his saving death and resurrection. In the Gospel we experience the humility of the Son of God washing his apostles' feet to prepare them for priesthood and the Eucharist. Lest they misunderstand his actions, he speaks plainly, "For I have set you an example, that you also should do as I have done to you" (John 13:15).

From the very beginning of Christianity the Eucharist has been the source of our unity and community in Christ. The house liturgies emphasized community in their familial sharing. When liturgies moved to church buildings, the ideal of sharing and participating in the worship continued. We are always called to the humility of the foot washing as well as the service to the poor and needy that it symbolized.

The Eucharist is a communion with the infinite love of the Lord Jesus that is poured into our hearts by the Holy Spirit. We are gradually transformed into Christ through years of sacramental celebration. We are not worthy, but Jesus still speaks the words of welcome in the Eucharist that sanctifies us.

Pray

Lord Jesus, let the Bread that is your body and that makes us one be also a Bread for the world, inspiring us to works of compassion, peace and justice. Amen.

Reflect

How do you participate in each Mass? What helps you benefit from the Eucharist? What is the link between the Mass and eucharistic adoration?

. . .

March 21

GOOD FRIDAY OF THE LORD'S PASSION

Isaiah 52:13—53:12; Hebrews 4:14–16; 5:7–9;
John 18:1—19:42

The Poor's Best Friend

They gather around a wooden, life-sized statue of Jesus, whose hands are chained to a pole and on whose body the wound marks can be seen. The statue portrays Jesus, not as an elegant figure, but as a simple peasant. Pilgrims place candles around him and talk to him as a friend. They stroke his face lovingly and tell him their problems. Some ask for cures or to be able to hear or see better. Others kiss his hands and his face and prostrate before him.[12]

The above poignant scene occurred during an annual Holy Week pilgrimage in rural Poland. One hundred fifty thousand people gathered to reenact the Passion of Christ. The photographer and author did not disclose the name of the place. It might be called the shrine of the poor in spirit.

In his first sermon Jesus applied to himself the words of

Isaiah, "The Spirit of the Lord…has anointed me to bring good news to the poor" (Luke 4:18). At the beginning of his Sermon on the Mount Jesus said, "Blessed are the poor in spirit, for theirs is the kingdom of heaven" (Matthew 5:3). Christ's good news and promise of blessedness and happiness was won in his death and resurrection.

Jesus became poor for us that we might become rich in grace. The tenth Station of the Cross shows him stripped of his clothing. He allowed himself to have his dignity torn away so he could experience the embarrassment of the homeless, the poor, the unjustly treated and all people at their wits' end whether materially rich or poor.

By his divine power he turned these tragic circumstances into a triumph of love and mercy. This is why the lonely and abandoned feel at home with him at the cross. He knows our sorrows and helps us to be healed. *Adoramus te, Christe.* We adore you, O Christ.

Pray

Crucified Lord, you urged us who labor and are burdened to come to you. You promised us that you would then give us rest, a peace beyond all human understanding. We adore you.

Reflect

Why do the poor love the Passion of Christ? Why does anyone who is poor in spirit come to the cross? How does the cross move you?

March 22
HOLY SATURDAY

Vigil: Genesis 1:1—2:2 or 1:1, 26-31a; Genesis 22:1–18 or
22:1–2, 9a, 10–13, 15–18; Exodus 14:15—15:1; Isaiah
54:5–14; Isaiah 55:1–11; Baruch 3:9–15, 32—4:4; Ezekiel
36:16–17a, 18–28; Romans 6:3–11; Matthew 28:1–10

A Blaze of Candles for the Baptized

As they emerge from the grace-giving womb of the font, a
blaze of candles burns brightly beneath the tree of faith. The
Easter festival brings the grace of holiness from heaven to
men.[13]

One of the joyful facts about the Easter Vigil is that annually
over 150,000 people become Catholic either through baptism
or full communion with the church. That is a tribute to the
evangelizing witness of parishes, couples and other faith-filled
people. It also testifies to the effectiveness and maturity of the
Rite of Christian Initiation of Adults (RCIA) and of children
(RCIC).

Growth inspires us, especially when it is solidly based on
faith, stability and continuity. The ultimate cause of such
growth is the fruit of Christ's saving death and resurrection
and the power of the Holy Spirit whom Jesus promised to send
us. The graces that flow from Calvary and the empty tomb are
awesome and have been yielding millions of faithful believers
for every century since the time of Christ. The love that the
Holy Spirit pours into Christian hearts from the first three
thousand at Pentecost (Acts 2:41) to the present is a visible
guarantee of the awesome power of Christ's redemption.

Now that Christ has given us all we need to live a Christian life, we should not let the distracting demands of anxiety and pride prevent us from being as much like our redeemer as possible. In everything Jesus did and suffered for our salvation, he desired his followers to share in the treasures he possessed.

Jesus has not restored us to the old paradise of Adam and Eve, but rather to participation in eternal life, the better paradise even here on earth. Our risen Lord does this especially in the Holy Eucharist, our heavenly bread. Sing with joy, "The Lord is risen! Alleluia!"

Pray
Alleluia! Praise to you, Risen Lord Jesus. In revealing yourself to Mary Magdalene, you confirmed her love for you. Increase our faith, hope and love and help us be living witnesses of your risen presence. Amen.

Reflect
How does your faith in Christ's resurrection affect your life? Why is Christ's resurrection essential for our salvation?

. . .

March 23

EASTER SUNDAY
The Resurrection of the Lord
Acts 10:34a, 37–43; Colossians 3:1–4 or Corinthians 5:6b–8;
John 20:1–9 or Matthew 28:1–10 or, at an afternoon or
evening Mass, Luke 24:13–35

It's God's Morning Again in the Church
There is a story told about the only white man buried in a cemetery for blacks. He lost his mother when he was a baby.

His father, who did not remarry, hired a black woman to raise his son. She took her job seriously. The motherless boy received warmhearted attention. He remembered often how Mandy bent over him in his bedroom each day and said, "Wake up, my boy, God's mornin' is come."

With the passing years Mandy remained his surrogate mother. When he came home from college, she climbed the stairs and woke him in the same way. One day after he became a distinguished statesman, he received the sad message, "Mandy is dead. Can you attend the funeral?" As he stood by her grave, he told his friends, "If I die before Jesus comes, I want to be buried here beside Mandy. I think on Resurrection Day she'll turn to me and say, 'Wake up, my boy, God's mornin' has come.'"[14]

In her tender way, Mandy repeated what Mary Magdalene said to the apostles at the first Easter. "Wake up my boys, Christ's mornin' has come." The apostles' faith was a bit groggy, slow to believe. Mary Magdalene witnessed the mysterious link between love and knowledge.

Jesus loved us so much that he kept the scars of love. Some might say, "Why didn't God fix him up? Why the scars?" Could it be that we only see Jesus when we can behold the wounds of love? Jesus is living but never fixed up. He is not bound by death, but he is scarred for eternity. The deaf have a sign for Jesus. They place the middle finger of their right hand into the palm of their left. The wound of love is Christ's name.

Pray

Risen Lord Jesus, I love you and thank you for the gift of your resurrection. Because of this our faith in you is possible. Help us witness to all you taught and did for us. Amen.

Reflect

What are some ways you find Christ's resurrection has an impact on your life? Why was it necessary for Christ to rise as well as die for our salvation?

. . .

Closing Meditation

For the sake of you, who left a garden, I was betrayed…in a garden, and I was crucified in a garden.

See on my face the spittle I received in order to restore to you the life I once breathed into you. See there the marks of the blows I received in order to refashion your warped nature in my image. On my back see the marks of the scourging I endured to remove the burden of sin that weighs upon your back. See my hands, nailed firmly to a tree, for you who once wickedly stretched out your hand to a tree….

My side has healed the pain in yours….

Rise, let us leave this place…. The bridal chamber is adorned, the banquet is ready, the eternal dwelling places are prepared, the treasure houses of all good things lie open. The kingdom of heaven has been prepared for you from all eternity.[15]

Notes

1. Paraphrased from St. John Chrysostom, Concerning the Statutes, Homily III on Fasting, Nicene Fathers, Volume 9, retrieved from http://www.orthodox.net/articles/orthodox-christian-fasting-john-chrysostom.html.

2. Austin Flannery, O.P., ed., *Vatican Council II: The Conciliar and Post Conciliar Documents,* vol. 1, *Lumen Gentium,* 40 (Northport: N.Y.: Costello, 1988), p. 397.

3. Saint Augustine of Hippo, *Confessions,* 10:27, Henry Chadwick, trans. (New York: Oxford University Press, 1998), p. 201.

4. Morris West, *The Devil's Advocate* (New York: Dell, 1959), p. 34.

5. Robert Bolt, *A Man for All Seasons* (New York: Random House, 1962), pp. 91–92.

6. Pope John Paul II, Homily at Giants Stadium, October 5, 1995, retrieved from http://www.usccb.org/mrs/pope.shtml.

7. Bolt, pp. 76–77.

8. Fyodor Dostoevsky, *The Brothers Karamazov,* Richard Pevear and Larissa Volokhonsky, trans. (New York: Farrar, Straus and Giroux, 1990).

9. Katherine Anne Porter, *Ship of Fools* (Mattituck, N.Y.: Amereon Limited, 1994).

10. E. Allison Peers, trans., *The Life of Teresa of Jesus: The Autobiography of Teresa of Avila* (New York: Doubleday, 1960), pp. 240–241.

11. Corpus Christi, Responsory, *The Liturgy of the Hours,* vol. 3 (New York: Catholic Book Publishing, 1975), p. 611.

12. Adam Bujak and Marjorie *Young Journeys To Glory: A Celebration of the Human Spirit* (New York: Harper and Row, 1976).

13. From an Easter Homily by an Ancient Author, *The Liturgy of the Hours,* vol. 2 (New York: Catholic Book Publishing, 1975), p. 583.

14. James S. Hewett, ed., *Illustrations Unlimited: A Topical Collection of Hundreds of Stories, Quotations, and Humor for Speakers, Writers, Pastors, and Teachers* (Carol Stream, Ill.: Tyndale House, 1988) pp. 163–164.

15. From an ancient homily on Holy Saturday, *The Liturgy of the Hours,* vol. 2, pp. 497–498.